NEVER A WASTED *Life*

From Backpacker to
Luxury Travel Designer
of the Year

DANIEL SALMON

Copyright © 2023 Dan Salmon

All rights reserved. No part of this book may be reproduced or used in any manner without the prior written permission of the copyright owner, except for the use of brief quotations in a book review.

To request permissions, contact the publisher at reservations@neverawastedjourney.com

The information in this book was correct at the time of publication, but the author does not assume any liability for loss or damage caused by errors or omissions.

ISBN:

Thank you to my Mum, Linda, for giving me such fantastic first tastes of travel from an early age (from the magic of Disneyland Paris to a fly-drive across America) and for supporting me through everything in life.

To my wife, Jo, for your understanding and putting up with me working weekends, taking late-night calls, and making last-minute changes to our plans. And to our three children, Harrison, Hendrix, and Savannah, for being the motivation for all I do in life.

Thank you to all my friends, other family members, and work colleagues who I have shared this adventure with so far.

And thanks to all of you who have booked with me and given me the pleasure of assisting with your holiday plans. Without you, none of this would be possible.

CONTENTS

1	My First Steps into The Wider World	1
2	Adventures Down Under	6
3	South Pacific Escapades	17
4	Asian Antics	23
5	Time To Get a Real Job	29
6	On Call for the Super Rich	38
7	Never a Wasted Journey	42
8	Wow-Factor Experiences	54
9	The Future of Travel	61
	About The Author	71
	My Little Heart Warrior	74

CHAPTER 1

My First Steps into The Wider World

If I hadn't fallen down a mountain when I was 19 years old, I wouldn't be where I am today.

I don't mean that literally – I'm not still stuck at the bottom, calling for help. But without my accident, I suppose I might still be up a mountain, teaching toddlers how to snowplough and surviving on a diet of dishes made almost entirely from melted cheese.

That had been the plan; after leaving school at 16, I'd headed off to Tignes and Val D'Isere to get my ski instructor qualifications. But it wasn't to be. An Eddie-the-Eagle-on-steroids incident ended my snowy dreams almost as soon as they'd begun, changing the entire direction of my life and setting me on the road to where I am today.

Now, I'm an award-winning luxury travel agent, booking trips of a lifetime for my stable of celebrity and high-net-worth clients. Mountains still play a part in my life, but they're just another location for the kind of extraordinary experiences that have become my bread-and-butter. I'm as likely to be setting up an underwater proposal in the Maldives or a private-jet pub crawl across the Australian outback as a high-altitude helicopter picnic on the summit of a glacier.

This book is about my journey from there to here; how a scared, shivering teenager with a dislocated shoulder ended up as the go-to travel consultant for the international jet set. The road has been long, winding, and sometimes bumpy; and I can't claim that I'm any less clumsy now than I was then. However, the mistakes I made as an accident-prone backpacker taught me valuable lessons about travelling and mean I can help my clients avoid these pitfalls themselves.

In these pages, you'll journey with me around the globe, having a good giggle at my many mishaps and perhaps getting a better understanding not only of each thrilling destination but also of me and how I can help make sure that not a single moment of your holiday is ever wasted.

It hasn't always been straightforward, to say the least – I'm definitely one of those people that things just… happen to. Even my journey home after my accident wasn't without incident. On my way to the airport, carrying all of my ski equipment, luggage, and travel documents with my one good arm, I dropped my wallet while waiting at the bus stop. My instant and instinctive reaction was to stretch out my leg and attempt to kick it back up into my hand. But in hindsight, that was a rather ambitious idea. Instead, I ended up missing my wallet completely and kicking my shoe off, which flew above me, over the top of the bus stop I was waiting in, and onto the roof of a bus travelling in the other direction. I was left hopping along in the snow and ice with one trainer on, swinging my arm that wasn't in a sling around to get the attention of the driver, to retrieve my wallet and be able to travel back home.

Despite this, I wasn't put off getting out on the open road again. My skiing dreams might have been shattered, but the travel bug had bitten me, badly, and I devoted myself to an alternative adventure – a gap year. After many months of planning and saving, my route was planned and my tickets booked, and I spent the following twelve months exploring China, Australia, New Zealand, Fiji, and Thailand.

Initially, I'd been going to travel with a friend, but due to a last-minute change, I found myself needing to build up the courage to do it all alone. Looking back, going ahead with this trip solo is the best thing I could ever have done – it made me the person I am today. It taught me so much, introduced me to many different types of people, and opened my eyes to different cultures. It's why I say if you ever have the chance to travel, do it!

I say this despite the fact my first big adventure came with plenty of ups and downs right from the get-go. Half asleep from my long flight to China, I mistook my shaving foam for deodorant in the airport bathroom and had to pass through customs looking like a shame-faced Mr Whippy. Then I hired a bike to explore Beijing, made a wrong turn as soon as I set off, and managed to take out a cluster of local cyclists in the process. I found myself returning to the safety of the hotel five minutes later to escape the angry mob. Katie Melua may have thought there were nine million bicycles in Beijing, but there were now nine million minus five.

But determined to experience authentic Chinese culture, I resisted the urge to spend my first night ordering the standard club sandwich and fries from the hotel room service menu and ventured out to explore local life. Following the delicious smells wafting through the backstreets, I discovered a small, low-key restaurant filled to the rafters with locals tucking into some delicious-looking dishes.

What could go wrong?

As soon as I walked in, all eyes were on me. Being six-foot-two and having blonde highlights meant I stood out like a sore thumb. The problem was that I didn't speak Mandarin, and the waitress didn't speak Essex, so after a game of charades and pointing at photos on their menu, I eventually ordered several dishes and nervously waited for what was to follow.

First up, Chinese soup. Or so I thought. I took a large mouthful, and despite my best efforts to swallow, I choked, spluttered, and sprayed a fountain all over the table in front of me. The other diners erupted in fits of laughter, and I realised I had taken a spoonful of the disinfectant-laced finger bowl designed to freshen up my hands between courses. Cue roaring laughter from surrounding tables at my expense, a washing up liquid-like taste in my mouth, bright red cheeks from embarrassment, and the beginning of a steep learning curve in international travel.

But despite the inauspicious start, I loved China. It was one of the most enthralling countries I have ever visited – a land of ancient traditions, captivating landscapes, and fascinating cultures. I walked along the Great Wall, visited the Forbidden City, explored art galleries and learned the history of Tiananmen Square – all as part of a brief stopover. With the inspiring Terracotta Warriors in Xi'an, the giant pandas of Chengdu, the magnificent Yangtze River, and the futuristic city of Shanghai still on my wish list, I plan to return one day.

But my next stop was Australia, where plenty more adventures – and mishaps – awaited.

CHAPTER 2

Adventures Down Under

To this day, the island continent remains one of my favourite destinations. Adventures are endless, from sailing around the Whitsunday Islands and diving in vivid coral reefs to climbing Sydney Harbour Bridge and driving the Great Ocean Road.

My first trip wasn't at all idyllic, however. Rather than sampling the finer things in life—which I have now become used to—my travels then involved moving from hostel to hostel (of a varying standard; some where cockroaches scurried across the floor), living off super noodles due to my non-existent cooking skills, and spending hour upon cramped hour aboard many a Greyhound Bus while travelling down the East Coast. However, this allowed me to put my savings into all the experiences I had on my Australian Bucket List and leave a trail of schooner beers and good friends at each stop.

The start of my adventure Down Under began in tropical North Queensland, in the city of Cairns, a haven for adventure-seekers and the gateway to two World Heritage-listed icons – the Great Barrier Reef and the Daintree Rainforest.

I had decided to fly up to Cairns from Sydney and then make my way down the coast by bus, ticking off my wish list locations along the way. However, halfway through this flight, the captain suddenly announced that we were going to have to divert to Brisbane Airport due to a technical issue on the aircraft. Technical issue? Nervously, we all tightened our seatbelts, held our armrests that little bit tighter, and counted down the minutes (which seemed like hours) until we were back on the ground once again.

As we descended towards Brisbane, I looked out of the window to see the flashing lights of two fire engines and a medical team waiting for us down below. As we bounced down the runway, they accelerated behind us, and I really began to wonder what was wrong with the plane. I was just looking forward to getting off, but no, instead, we waited and waited on board before the captain's voice returned, informing us that all was 'fixed' and we were 'ready to go' again. Ready to go?! I would have hoped at least for a replacement plane, but off we set back along the runway and back up into the skies.

I spent the next two hours in the air debating which was worse, the worry this plane was going to fall out of the sky at any minute or the bare, hairy, long-toe-nailed foot that was rubbing up against my shoulder as one of the passengers next to me gave her husband a foot massage.

At least Cairns, with its laidback atmosphere, was waiting for me, and I spent most of my days lazing on the Esplanade Lagoon's sandy shores and soaking up the sunshine. By evening I was under the spell of Cairns' thriving nightlife scene, which is home to many fantastic waterfront bars and restaurants.

One day, while mooching around the lagoon, I heard a shout, and to my surprise, I looked up to see two cheeky grins: my friends from the UK, Tom and Jo. Their familiar faces were a flavour of home, and we managed to spend a few days catching up. But one particular night didn't end as we planned; the weather changed to a tropical storm and Tom's face changed just as quickly to a panicked frenzy, realising that he had left the roof of their campervan open. It was too late to do anything, so we sunk a few more beers and they spent the night sleeping on a soggy, wet-through mattress.

Diving in Headfirst

What have I gone and done now? I thought to myself as the small plane I was on bounced around in the clouds as it made its way up to 14,000 feet. I had decided to test my boundaries and signed up for a skydive but was immediately regretting my decision as my knees began to shake with fear.

"Go! Go! Go!" radioed the pilot, and then it was my turn to jump. I slowly crawled towards the open side door, finding myself sitting on the side of the aircraft with my legs dangling over the side, looking down at the ant-sized landmarks below. One deep breath, a lean forward, and there was no going back.

What followed was a 60-second, 110-mile-per-hour, adrenalin-fuelled experience of a lifetime. If you are ever going to do a skydive, make sure it's here – the views of lush rainforest, the reef, and the expansive ocean are quite simply breath-taking.

Not every jumper had quite such a positive experience; my instructor shared stories of one gentleman losing his false teeth during a jump and another whose false eye popped out and rolled around and around in his goggles all the way down. Not quite the same view to write home about for him…

Looking for something a little less stressful, I visited the beautiful, untouched Cape Tribulation and the Daintree Rainforest where I swam under waterfalls and came face-to-face with saltwater crocodiles, brown tree snakes, green tree frogs, and beautifully coloured kingfisher birds while cruising along the mangrove-lined river.

It was soon time for me to move on from Cairns, but Queensland's natural splendours did not end there and one of my most memorable adventures was to follow.

Sadly, my dad passed away when I was just five and although he is dearly missed, I have very fond memories of sailing on our boat through the Balearic Islands when he was still with us.

So, when the opportunity came to sail through the Whitsunday Islands I jumped at the chance – literally! In Airlie Beach, I made my way down to the marina to join my fellow passengers on a 27-foot ex-racing boat, which would be our home for the following five days.

"G'day me old cobber! Jump in," instructed the crew member waiting in the dinghy ten feet below, ready to take us across to our yacht.

And so, I did, quite literally. With one big step, I jumped off the jetty and down towards his open arms. The worried look on his face suddenly made me realise I had made a drastic mistake – he'd intended me to take the steps. Instead, I bounced down into—and then quickly out of—the dinghy. There followed a tremendous splash, and I was floating face down in the water, fully clothed and with my large backpack keeping me afloat. Despite my previous lifeguard training, I found myself needing saving, and I had to make my introductions to the other guests looking like a drowned rat.

I was lucky to be in fantastic company throughout, with four couples from all corners of the world and another singleton who was from Japan. Although he didn't speak any English and I didn't speak any Japanese, we stuck together, made conversation charades-style, and got on well, all things considered.

Anchor up and away we set. Over the next few days, we explored lush islands with sun-kissed beaches and coral reefs under the clearest waters filled with exotic marine life. By day, we dived and snorkelled with vibrant coloured fish, turtles, rays, and sharks. By night we wined, dined, and shared stories as the sound of a guitar echoed across the waves, while the sky lit up with incredible sunsets and shooting stars.

Though I'd previously dived the Great Barrier Reef from Cairns (plus the Red Sea in Egypt and various wrecks scattered throughout Europe), this was different; away from the crowds and simply incredible.

Yet all my experience counted for nothing after one early morning dive when I attempted to remove my wetsuit. Disaster struck as I got my foot stuck at the final stages of removal and hopped around the top deck, from one side to the other, like a headless chicken. Everyone jumped out of my way looking for cover, and as the safety lines on the side of the boat got closer, I took a leap of faith to try and clear them. My jump wasn't high enough, and as my body went overboard, my wetsuit became tangled in the wires. There I was, dangling off the side of the boat, bouncing up and down on the world's smallest bungee jump. Not having quite got to grips with my sea legs, I was relieved to learn that the rest of the day would be spent exploring beautiful Whitehaven Beach, renowned as one of the best in the world.

After hiking through the rainforest, we found our way to a lookout where we were greeted by a feast of a view – endless shades of blue waters, pristine snow-white beaches and not a single other person to be seen. The sand was as soft as cotton wool and the ocean crystal clear. As we lazed and swam in the bath-warm water, baby sharks and rays frolicked, and pods of dolphins playfully leapt out of the water further offshore. As the day ended, we were reluctant to leave, but it was time to moor up for our last evening together.

We couldn't have picked a better location. A whale and her calf played in the water just metres away and the most incredible sunset sunk slowly into the vast ocean. A feast followed under the starlit sky, and we drank our way into the early hours. One of Australia's most famous backpacker drinks is known as 'goon' and is basically four litres of cheap wine drunk from a carton. When reading the side of the box, you will find it is cheap for a reason, with traces of egg, nuts, and fish on the ingredients list. One box down, I looked around with one eye open to realise it was just myself and my Japanese friend still up, so we decided to call it a night.

By this time, it was pitch black and we had only the moonlight to help us navigate to our bunk beds below deck. My new bestie led the way, and I followed close behind. Glancing over his shoulder to make sure I was still with him; he was suddenly taken aback to discover I was nowhere to be seen. Assuming I'd fallen overboard (again), in a panic, he shouted to alert the crew, who, despite being half-asleep, shot up to the top deck. Assuming I was 'man overboard' for the second time on the voyage, they searched the ocean with torches and life rings in hand. But where was I?

I am pleased to say I wasn't in the cold, dark waters surrounding the boat, but had taken a detour in another direction. A South Korean couple in the group had decided to spend their last night sleeping with a calming ocean breeze blowing through their cabin's open roof hatch. As I had attempted to make my way back to my own bunk, I had instead fallen through their hatch, landing on them both in bed and completely ruining their romantic evening. All three of us were scared stiff and our high-pitched screams echoed across the waves as we tried to work out what had just happened – an attempt not helped by the language barrier.

It was definitely time to move on to the next adventure.

A Crash Landing
Over the next few months, I made my way down the coast. Fraser Island gave me my Bear Grills fix; all harsh rainforest, deadly dingos, and tiger shark-infested waters. The Gold Coast brought a mix of lazy beach days, great nightlife, and fun-filled theme parks. (Although I now know better than to book the Disney lunch for an adult travelling alone, as it was a tad embarrassing to show up for a meet-

and-greet character experience and realise I was at least 15 years older than anyone else in the group). I gained my Advanced PADI scuba diving qualification in Byron Bay, then headed for Sydney.

"Uh oh!" It was my first morning in Sydney, and I realised I had made a drastic error – again.

I was staying with a good friend from back home and her two housemates. Rather than wake them early after our first night on the town catching up, I quietly made my way out onto the balcony to get some fresh air. Wanting to be sure I didn't disturb my hosts, I pulled the glass sliding door behind me. What I hadn't realised was that it would automatically lock, and I was now stranded on the balcony in just my boxer shorts and in full view of the neighbours making their way to work on their morning commutes.

With the bedrooms being on the other side of the building and nobody acknowledging my panicked knocking on the glass door to get back in, I tried an Action Man-esque manoeuvre, climbing over the first-floor balcony rail and hanging with my legs dangling for a few seconds before plucking up the courage to let go and drop to the ground, metres below. After a fall and a crash into a bush, I brushed myself off and raised my head to see a young family looking back at me from their breakfast table, eyes and mouths wide open.

After crash-landing into Sydney life, I based myself there for a good few months, cleaning cars for Audi and serving tables in a coffee shop to top up my funds. All the while, I maximised my free time to create fantastic memories along the way, from rolling out my towel and soaking up Sydney's laid-back beach lifestyle in Bondi and Manly to people-watching and exploring the cafes and bars of Darling Harbour and the Rocks.

I took walks through the Royal Botanical Gardens, adventurous treks through the Blue Mountains, heard live music from the buskers down by the waterfront of Circular Quay, jumped on a ferry across to Taronga Zoo and grabbed a sundowner with a view of the Opera House and Harbour Bridge in the background. I saw the city from the waves during an adrenaline-filled power boat ride and from above on a Sydney Harbour Bridge climb. The sheer achievement felt as satisfying as the panorama unfolding beneath my feet – the waterfront, the Opera House, and views stretching from the Pacific Ocean to the Blue Mountains.

Aches and Pains

My final stop on my adventure Down Under was Melbourne, and I turned my trip into a homage to the sporting venues I had seen on TV back home, visiting the Olympic Stadium, the Rod Laver Arena, and the MCG, where I got to follow in the footsteps of many cricketing greats by walking onto the famous turf.

I'd also timed my trip to link in with the Melbourne Grand Prix, and the atmosphere was electric with the Red Arrows and Australian Air Force tumbling across the sky above, while down below the noise and speed of the race were thrilling.

After the race, I took part in the circuit walk,

joining thousands of other fans in walking the bends of the circuit and over the starting grid, getting a glimpse into the pit lane. As I did so, I noticed the odd snigger and finger pointing in my direction — it was like Beijing all over again but this time I had no idea why. As I hopped on the bus back to the city centre, I finally realised. Glancing in the driver's mirror, I saw my reflection resembling a human tomato from wearing no sun cream throughout the whole day.

To top it all off, as I got off the bus, something dropped from the opening door onto my neck. My instinct to whip it off with my hand resulted in this something—which turned out to be a spider—defending itself and biting down into my skin. Now I didn't just have the worry of my burns, but also the paranoia of having been bitten by an Australian spider.

My final evening was spent soothing my Rudolph-like nose, grilled forearms, and glowing calves. Then the swelling from the bite began and I drifted off to sleep wondering if I would make it through the night. The good news is that I did, but the bad news was that my time in Australia had come to an end.

CHAPTER THREE

South Pacific Escapades

I'd often gazed longingly at images of far-flung and secluded South Pacific islands. So, seeking downtime on warmer shores, I included Fiji in my itinerary. After stepping off the plane, I soon found myself bouncing over–and getting drenched by– waves en route to my first island stop via a small wooden boat. I was amazed it could even float, let alone travel at such speeds, but miraculously it survived the journey. I was greeted by a traditional communal dance and open arms from the locals, who remain some of the friendliest people I have ever come across.

The island was the location for the Brooke Shields film *The Blue Lagoon* and it was the perfect location to maroon myself for a few days. Here, the world seemed to move at an indolent pace – all white sands, ocean breezes, and endless colourful fish. A far cry from my local beach at home, Southend-On-Sea really paled in comparison.

Lazy days were spent trekking through tropical

jungle to isolated beaches where we played games, dozed in hammocks, and snorkelled on the reefs. I quickly bonded with the other guests on the island, and we remain firm friends to this day. By night, we feasted on local delicacies, sampled 'Kava' (the local firewater) under the star-filled sky and cheered on the fire walkers braving the burning ashes.

One of my fellow islanders was a character we nicknamed Captain Jack – a dead ringer for Jack Sparrow from the *Pirates of the Caribbean* movies. He got in the true island spirit and one afternoon, rather than heading for the beach to go snorkelling with us, he joined the locals for a bottle of rum.

It turned out he'd made the safer choice. After venturing out 300 metres offshore, we all suddenly found ourselves trapped. I thought it had been shallower than previous days and, indeed, we had massively misjudged the tide and soon found ourselves tucking our stomachs in, arching our bodies back and attempting to avoid the razor-sharp corals which were just centimetres below us. It was all to no avail – our knees, shins, and stomachs were shredded and with sharks not too far away, we decided that was enough snorkelling for one day and limped back to camp.

There was no sign of Captain Jack and thinking he must have headed home before the sun set, we made the half-hour trek through the jungle back to dinner, expecting to find him ready and waiting–if not slightly intoxicated–at the table. But the captain wasn't there. One hour passed, then another, and another, still with no sign of him. It was now pitch black and we began to worry. But then we heard a shout of "Ahoy, me hearties!" and there he was, staggering towards us with his now empty bottle of rum and a wide smile. He had found a quiet corner of the beach and fallen asleep in a hammock. Upon waking in a somewhat confused state, he had spent four hours attempting to find his bearings through the jungle, drunk as a skunk and in complete darkness. At least he was with us once again – even if he did attempt to eat his soup with a fork.

Submarine Scare
Our next Fijian experience was a three-night sailing trip through the Yasawa Islands. Our vessel was a large adventure boat, and my company the friends I had made over the previous few days. By day, we would relax in the sun, play games in the ocean, and eat delicious local cuisine. Come evening, it was sundowners on the top deck as we soaked up our surroundings, shared stories from all our travels so far, and attempted night fishing off the back of the boat. With piranhas being the catch of the evening, midnight swimming was off the menu!

As the cruise went on, our confidence grew, and we created our own mini-Olympics, diving from the top deck down into the ocean twenty metres below. There were many belly flops and lost bikinis, but these were exceeded by laughs along the way.

Next, it was time for a game of catch while treading water a little way from the boat. One misjudged throw and I had to swim around ten metres away from the boat to retrieve our ball. Suddenly, a shriek echoed across the waves and one of the girls on board was frantically screaming and pointing in my direction. My immediate fears were Jaws-themed, but the reality wasn't much better. I looked down to see a metre-long jellyfish gliding underneath me, its poisonous tentacles just inches from giving me a sharp sting. Then I saw another, and another, and another. We had chosen to play amongst a gigantic smack of jellyfish. Each one of us manoeuvred in and out of these creatures at a snail-like pace, before finding a clear channel and swimming for the boat as fast as we could. We were certainly ready for happy hour cocktails as soon as we were back on board.

Legendary Locations
Although each day in Fiji felt relaxed, our time there seemed over as soon as it had begun, and I headed for my next adventure – New Zealand. Through the contacts I have built up over the years, I am now able to create real bucket list experiences throughout the destination, with my favourite being the picnic of a lifetime I organised for two of my best clients. They flew by helicopter from their exclusive lodge to the coast for an early-morning fishing trip, then took off and headed for a local market accompanied by their own private chef, before finally landing on a glacier to have their selection all cooked for them and a picnic lunch served surrounded by some of the most breath-taking scenery on the planet.

Things were rather different on my first visit. Instead of flitting around by helicopter, we made our way through New Zealand cramped into a camper van, driving by day and sleeping swaying up on the top deck by night, rocked by the winter winds that picked up each evening. Our cuisine throughout the trip also involved trying every flavour of pot noodle ever created.

Our first stop was Matamata, home to the *Lord of the Rings* film set. All being fans, we looked forward to exploring. Upon our arrival at the Hobbit Village, we were welcomed by the owners of the estate, and what an estate to be proud of – acres and acres of rolling hills, mighty trees, and mirror lakes. The son of the family who owned this beautiful corner of New Zealand shared the story of how their home was chosen to be the location for the films.

The film producers had searched long distances by air across the country, looking for the perfect setting. Having spotted it, a team of producers raced along the dusty road leading to the main house. Once they got there, the father answered their excited knocks on his door. They told him their reason for being there and that he could expect a very substantial amount of money. His reaction was rather unexpected.

"Lord of what? Bugger off! I'm watching the rugby; you'll have to come back another day." Luckily, his son managed to talk him round, and, as a result, an iconic movie franchise was born. We all had great fun exploring the set and following in the footsteps of Frodo Baggins and Gandalf.

Geysers and Glow-Worms

Having felt colder than a polar bear's toenail since arriving in New Zealand (I'd now recommend clients visit during the summer months), we drove on to Rotorua, which our guidebook informed us was 'a geothermal wonderland with bubbling mud pools and natural hot springs'. As soon as we arrived at our camp for the evening, the ignition was quickly turned off, doors locked, and we all found ourselves warming up in the toasty waters under the stars.

Another world met us below Waitomo, with an amazing maze of limestone caves lined with galaxies of glow-worms, which we explored by boat. With six sheep to every person in New Zealand, I won't be disappointed if I don't see another one for the rest of my life, but I will miss the lush green Waikato countryside and incredible scenery that we drove through on our way to The Bay of Islands, a paradise of golden beaches and charming towns.

Our final stop, Auckland, offered an electric mix of cafes, restaurants, and buzzing nightlife. The time before my next flight had ticked down too quickly to explore the beautiful South Island, but I resolved to return one day for more adventures among the glaciers, mountains, and fjords.

CHAPTER FOUR
Asian Antics

Touch down in the final country I had included in my gap year – Thailand. I soon found myself aboard the night train down to Southern Thailand, settling into my seat with a fourteen-hour journey ahead. Rather than sweating on the daytime service in the scorching heat, I'd opted for the sleeper train, which was a little more expensive but promised a more comfortable journey. The conductor on the platform guided me to the train, and I made my way to my seat, stored my backpack away, and settled in, looking forward to a fun adventure ahead. Feeling a little peckish, I looked through the menu on offer, but quickly decided to decrease my chances of food poisoning by opting for a bottle of Sang Som instead.

As the train made its way out of the station, I sat back and poured myself my first plastic cup of rum. I soon realised how cold it was on board. A rickety fan swayed backwards and forwards, blasting the cold, dust-filled air through the carriage. Having previously been sitting on the platform with the warm Thai sun on my face, I was soon shivering like I had been transported to the Arctic.

To warm the cockles, I poured myself another rum, and another. A little way into the journey, the stewards made their way through and turned our seats into beds by pulling them down from the ceiling. This narrow bunk was hardly a king-size bed at The Ritz, and I began to wonder how I was going to get a wink of sleep, especially as the rattly window didn't shut out one bit of noise. But I reminded myself that this was all about the experience, so I pulled the motheaten door curtain across for some privacy, snuggled underneath a blanket, and watched the world go by out the window.

I was woken early by other passengers stumbling past still half asleep and the stewards looking to convert the bunks back into seats. Toothbrush in hand, I staggered towards the bathroom. Any idea of freshening up disappeared as I was hit with a wall of stench – the mix of a squat toilet and a fourteen-hour journey had taken its toll. Instead, I headed for the completely open door in between the connecting carriages and sat down on the steps to clear my fuzzy head and watch the rising sun come up over the surrounding countryside.

This seemed a great idea until the train swayed violently, and I found myself lurching towards the tracks below. As the train continued to speed along, I flailed backwards with one arm and luckily clenched onto the handrail, stopping myself from falling off the train in the middle of nowhere. That seemed like enough fresh air for me, so I headed back to my seat to take in the safer view from behind the glass window until we pulled into the station.

After months of hostels, boats, campervans, and now trains, I took the chance to enjoy the incredible value Thai hotels offer. My bar was lower then, with a fridge, a private bathroom, my own tv, and air conditioning; I couldn't believe my luck!

I have since returned to Thailand, bedding down in jungle lodges in the north, visiting the elephants and temples and soaking up the local culture.

I've stayed at luxury hotels in Bangkok, enjoying dinner and cocktails from their rooftop bars, and I've lounged on the beaches of Krabi, with the finest sands and crystal-clear waters I've ever come across. But on this first trip, at the end of my gap year, funds wouldn't stretch to the luxury pool villas and treetop dining I now arrange for my clients.

Bars and Beaches
Phuket was my first experience of what Southern Thailand had to offer, and although it now caters for everyone from backpackers to billionaires, back then it was very different. If your image of Phuket was ever seedy bars, scammers, and ladyboys, back then you would have been absolutely right.

"When in Rome," I thought to myself as I jumped on the back of a moped and headed into town. I passed other mopeds resembling an acrobatic stunt team with six people all piled onto one bike – one way to keep the costs down when splitting the fare.

Heading for the bright lights and pumping music of the bars, I sunk cocktails and danced on the tables, even plucking up the Dutch courage to sample the food on offer from a local street vendor – although don't ask me what it was, to this day, I'm still unsure.

Although I loved a good night out (as I'm sure you've worked out by now), I wanted to see what the other side of Phuket offered, too. Maya Bay is better known as the location of the film *The Beach*, and although it was incredibly impressive to look at, it was too packed with tourists to enjoy. In 2018, the area was completely closed to restore the nature, wildlife, and corals, and has recently reopened with new guidelines limiting tourists and protecting the environment, which I think is a fantastic idea. To find somewhere a little less crowded back then, we headed for Phi Phi Don, a relaxing spot with incredible snorkelling and tempting hammocks to while away the afternoon.

Before I left, I wanted to fit in one last trip and, being a big 007 fan, it had to be James Bond Island, the location of *The Man with the Golden Gun*. I followed in the footsteps of Sir Roger Moore, exploring everything I had seen in the film as a young boy, with the background of limestone mountains towering over the emerald-green waters. It was all going so well, but in the split second it would have taken Roger to raise an eyebrow, those tranquil blue skies turned a dramatic dark shade of grey. Then, it was a race against time to get back to the mainland before the rain started.

Too late. The heavens well and truly opened and in Thailand, when it rains, it pours! We rocked from side to side in our longboat, bouncing over the gigantic waves, scooping out water that had come over the sides with our water bottles. Everyone onboard was convinced we were going to either sink or capsize. With huge relief when we made it back to the waiting jetty, the chaos wasn't over. Inexplicably, a monkey clambered onto my head and then down onto my chest, where it became evident it had somehow confused me for its mother and was trying to suckle – a very bizarre moment to cap off a tumultuous trip.

City Sights and Souvenirs
After a visit to Ko Pha Ngan for the world-famous Full Moon Party, and much-needed recovery time on the beautiful Koh Samui with its soft sand beaches, lush tropical jungle, and hidden waterfalls, I headed for bustling Bangkok, where the weather

was sweltering. (I've learnt from my mistake and now send clients in the cooler months!).

Arriving in the scorching afternoon, I put the tourist sites I wanted to visit on hold and headed for the air-conditioned mall and some last-minute Christmas shopping for family back home. Even though I didn't have many baht left, Thailand's incredible value for money (and my now-honed bartering skills) meant I ended up laden with bags.

Climbing into the back of one of the tuk-tuks waiting out front, I piled my bags on top of me and sat back to enjoy the ride back to my hotel. Who am I kidding? I hung on for dear life as my rider cycled in and out of cars, dodged pedestrians, and responded to every horn beeped in our direction with a loud shout and a wave of his hand in return. I regained my nerve enough to venture out and visit the floating markets, temples, and glittering Grand Palace, making the most of this final stopover before it was time to return to England – and find myself a job.

CHAPTER FIVE

Time To Get a Real Job

I'd learnt many things during my gap year, not least that I wanted a career in the travel industry. I soon found myself working in the flagship store for one of the UK's biggest travel companies. My new office was on High Street Kensington, with its supercars, smart streets, and super-rich residents. The trade-off for this glamorous location was that my lunches each week cost as much as my pay cheque.

With just my experience of travelling the world on my CV, no higher educational qualifications, and no experience working in sales, I owe everything to the lady who took the risk of giving me my first role. Elspeth headed our 'Dream Team' and along with six other ladies, it was a role that I really enjoyed. Yes, I was the only guy in the store and that meant being the tea boy, doing the breakfast run, hearing the daily gossip, and being a shoulder to cry on, but it was a fantastic team and we all got on so well – working hard by day and socialising with just as much commitment by night. With a parking space renting for a six-figure sum and houses selling for tens of millions of pounds, holiday budgets were impressive, and one customer, in particular, did me an unwitting favour.

"Congratulations Dan, you are the winner of our global incentive! Get your bags packed," said an excited American voice on the other end of the phone.

"That's fantastic news! Thank you so much," I replied.

Truthfully, I had no idea that there was an incentive running, what I'd won, or where I was heading, but it turned out I'd really hit the jackpot. I had sold a particular suite at a well-known hotel in the Bahamas and was automatically entered into a draw for travel agents from across the world. Lady Luck was on my side and I won a VIP all-expenses paid trip to the Champions League Final in Rome. Business Class flights, a luxury hotel, behind-the-scenes access to the Vatican, a private tour of the Colosseum, meals in the very best restaurants, a private meet-and-greet with one of my favourite sporting personalities –the greatest referee in history, Pierluigi Collina–and the best seats in the house for the final between Manchester United and Barcelona. Being single at the time, my good friend James accompanied me on this trip of a lifetime, and he still owes me to this day.

As a big West Ham fan who suffered years of relegations and heartbreaks, being able to watch players like Ronaldo and Messi on the same pitch was a nice change and an experience I will never forget. It also gave me a moment of clarity and I knew this was exactly what I wanted to do with my life – not just book holidays, but create incredible, one-of-a-kind experiences that would stay in my clients' memories for a lifetime, too.

I firmly believe that if you don't travel or don't love travelling, you shouldn't be working in the industry. You must love it or you're in the wrong job. I had that in abundance and a passion for sharing it with every single person who walked in off the high street needing help with their travel plans.

So, I put my head down and worked hard, learning more each day. Luckily, the company that I worked for specialised in tailor-made luxury holidays across the world and I was given access to educational trips that took me to some incredible places, from a flying safari through Namibia and jeep dune bashing in Dubai to Orangutan spotting in Borneo, partying at the Rio Carnival, and trekking the Inca Trail in Peru.

But even though I was now travelling in a more luxurious style, my trips still managed to contain a few eventful moments. My first welcome to the honeymooners' paradise of the Maldives was not the dreamy, tranquil experience I had imagined.

"Put your life jackets on and get to the back of the boat!" bellowed the captain as the crew ran around in a panicked frenzy. Fellow passengers were vomiting into their duty-free carrier bags as the rest of us hung onto our seats for dear life.

Despite landing under overcast skies, the boat transfer to our island resort went ahead as planned, and we were told that there would only be 'the odd bumpy wave or two'. The odd one? What followed was wave after giant wave, bouncing the boat high out of the ocean and smashing it back down again. The crew were scrambling all over the deck, trying to stay on their feet, water was pouring in through the seals of the windows, and I sincerely believed the boat was going to sink at any minute.

A ninety-minute 'pleasant' boat transfer turned into three hours of pure hell. What is it with me and boats? Normally speedboat transfers to resorts are nothing like this. However, this stretch of water was apparently renowned for high waves and rough journeys when the weather is bad. Nice of them to share that with us before we booked! As my fellow passengers and I staggered down the jetty one thing was for sure – we'd all be taking the seaplane option back.

Once the weather had cleared up, it was easy to get into the true Maldivian spirit. Don't let my first transfer put you off – it's truly one of the most breath-taking locations on the planet. Pure white sands, crystal clear waters, the ultimate in relaxation, and a diver's paradise with incredible marine life below the waves.

The toughest choice in the Maldives is whether to stay in a beach villa just yards from the water's edge or in a water villa on stilts above the ocean. I had the latter and made my way down the steps of my villa to spend hours snorkelling with tropical fish, baby sharks, and even turtles. The evenings were filled with beach barbecues and cocktails accompanied by live music. This really was the ultimate escape.

I got the bug and have since visited more than ten other islands, so my personal feedback (both good and bad) will make sure your stay is perfect – no storm-washed boat transfers for you! Instead, you'll enjoy private picnics on deserted islands, overwater spa treatments, diving with whale sharks, and sunset cruises amidst pods of playful dolphins.

Trail Fail

It may sound as if my travels were constantly chaotic, but most trips passed smoothly. I slid down Namibian dunes on a sand-board and flew low over the vast Namib-Naukluft desert without any emergency landings. In Dubai, I rode camels, flew in helicopters, and even skied indoors without a repeat of my earlier accident.

But in Peru, my luck changed and, once again, there was a little more drama than I'd intended…

For years, I had seen images of the mist-cloaked mountains, cloud-drenched forests and ancient ruins of the iconic Inca Trail, with the reward being Machu Picchu–the ancient citadel the Spanish never found–and I knew it was something I had to witness in person. After a few days of acclimatising in Cusco, we set off on our four-day trek. Backpack thrown over my shoulder, hiking boots laced, and with my flask of water in hand, I followed our guide and watched open-mouthed as our porters nimbly sped ahead, despite being burdened with all the cooking equipment, tents, sleeping bags, food and refreshments.

The first day flew by as we hiked through some of the most beautiful scenery in South America – waterfalls, rivers, panoramic mountain-top views, and charming local villages. We had been warned to take it easy on our first day, but I felt fine and couldn't work out why the rest of the group kept stopping to rest. I stuck doggedly to the guide's heels and the gap between myself and the rest began to get bigger and bigger. Maybe this should have been a sign to slow down. Even so, the porters were far ahead and by the time we reached the end of our day's hike, a fire was already set up, hot chocolates were served, and the cook was working his magic with delicious smells flowing through camp.

As the rest of the group trickled in and sat down to an alfresco dinner under the stars, I was curled up in my tent with the worst headache I have ever had. I had climbed too fast and the swift change in altitude was hitting me hard. It felt as if someone was continuously hitting me round the head with one of the porter's hiking poles. I closed my eyes and drifted off to sleep, hoping the feeling would pass. I must have been asleep for a good few hours before I suddenly woke up, knowing I was about to vomit. I clambered out of my tent, unable to see a thing due to the pitch-black darkness around me, tripping over rocks, falling into divots in the ground, and eventually landing in a giant puddle. It seems I'd learned nothing from my first night in Sydney – I was once again in just my boxers. Eventually I crawled back into my tent, put on every item of clothing from my backpack to warm up and drifted back off to sleep, hoping to wake up with a fresher head.

Sadly, when I woke up, things hadn't changed, and so the decision was made that I should be taken down off the mountain. My Inca Trail Trek was over after just the first day. Along with me came Tim, the good friend I had persuaded to come on the trip, who was now worrying about what on earth he was going to tell my mum if he didn't get me home in one piece. Completely out of it, I was hoisted up onto a donkey and we set off on the steep, slippery path, with Tim and one of our porters on foot.

At one point, there was no alternative but for me to walk too, and I collapsed on the floor with my body shaking and my eyes rolling back in my head. I was drifting in and out of consciousness and all I can remember is a panicked Tim yelling and running around demanding for a helicopter to be flown in to pick us up, plus a number of locals chanting a prayer and rubbing an antidote over my body to bring me round. I thought I was a goner!

Eventually I came round, and it was back on the donkey for a further few hours. By now we were still in the middle of nowhere with darkness creeping in. Poor Tim slumped down on the ground, weary and footsore, soaked to the skin from falling while crossing a fast-flowing river and burned to a crisp from the sun beating down for hours on his bald head. He couldn't go a step further. Luckily, having come down to a lower altitude, I was actually feeling a lot better, though I hadn't mentioned this as I was rather enjoying my donkey ride. We loaded Tim onto the donkey and I finished the last few miles on foot. Reaching the end felt like a lottery win, and I've never been so glad to see a hotel bed.

While I felt better the next morning, poor Tim was in a terrible state, with bad blisters on his feet and a sunburnt head. The local doctor told us he needed medication injected each day, and rather than pay the exorbitant charge for him to return, I volunteered to do it myself. Something I immediately regretted when I learned I needed to stick a needle in my best mate's backside.

After a few days of recovering, we agreed that we hadn't travelled all this way to miss out on seeing one of the wonders of the world, so we caught up with the rest of the group and visited Machu Picchu. This time by a combination of bus and train rather than hiking our way there as they did. The view of the lost city of the Incas was so spectacular it made up for the eventful journey, and I have since sent clients to reprise my journey without any problems – I learned the lesson of taking the first day slowly the hard way.

Despite some incredible trips and after three fantastic years, I realised I had come as far as I could in that role. I didn't want to get into management and with no other signs of progression, I needed to make my next move. The two-hour commute (each way) on a train every day wouldn't be missed, but the people would, and I still have a soft spot for all things Kensington.

CHAPTER SIX

On Call for The Super Rich

My next job wasn't much closer to home – the Oxford Street location only allowed an extra twenty minutes in bed each day. But, yet again, I loved it, and it was a pivotal step on my journey. I was taken on by one of the world's leading concierge companies, looking after the account holders of major banks, high net-worth individuals, sports personalities, and celebrities. The vision of the company was to help its members enjoy life hassle-free and that included everything from priority access to the best restaurants, shows, and events around the world to arranging dog walkers and purchasing gifts on behalf of clients for special occasions. I was in their travel department and thanks to my previous experience, qualified to look after the VIP members.

What was different about this role—and what I've continued to offer those who book with me to this day—was a real focus on getting the client more for their money; exclusive savings on hotels and flights worldwide, room upgrades, welcome amenities, and complimentary experiences while away. Anyone can book a holiday online, but these insider advantages are exactly why my clients come to me for help again and again.

While my Kensington customers had booked some pretty spectacular holidays, I took it to another level. One of my first bookings was for an individual only popping up the road to Scotland – but still spending £80,000 to do so. Where once I might have booked upgraded flights and private transfers, I was now reserving private jets and helicopter flights. I secured exclusive use of historic castles, organised private chefs to lay on Wagyu beef dinners, scheduled supercars for self-drive and negotiated trout-fishing in renowned lochs. This was my introduction to the detailed planning that is needed to create such fantastic trips, showing me how indispensable my book of contacts would become and how to go about packaging everything together in one seamless wrapper, so clients only notice the wow-factor and not the workings underneath.

It also showed me that for high-net-worth individuals, convenience is everything. Clients could contact me directly on my personal number and not have to wait on hold, go through endless automated systems, or fit in with restricted opening times. I have always understood that people lead busy lives and that their free time is precious. Some requests were rather unexpected – car hire in the Maldives; more toilet paper to be sent up to someone sitting on 'the throne' in their suite in

Dubai; one person even asked to speak to "Mr Kind Regards" after mistaking my email signature for my name. No day working in travel is boring.

Playing Hard; Working Harder

Sometimes a little boredom would even be welcome. When world events have sent travel into a tailspin, my job has been extra stressful, but I always make sure I'm there to look after my clients.

My first experience of this was the ash cloud of 2010 and the biggest closure of airspace since the Second World War. With ten million travellers stranded or unable to board flights, I stepped in to help those that had booked through our company and fuelled by caffeine, I worked throughout the night to make alternative arrangements. I finally stepped out for a 'lunch break' at 3am and passed by the street cleaners tidying up from the previous day's shoppers and party revellers. While many travellers slept on airport floors, I negotiated additional hotel nights free of charge for my clients, and arranged to get them home via boat, rail, and road, all while keeping their worried family members updated on their behalf.

More recently, I have hand-delivered travel documents during the 'Beast from the East' snowstorm which brought our postal service to a standstill and made last-minute changes to travel plans due to failed PCR tests during the COVID-19 pandemic, including on Boxing Day and New Year's Eve.

There are, however, many perks to working in the industry. During those years, I explored the shores of many more countries, from wine-tasting and safari in South Africa and snorkelling with turtles and hiking waterfalls in Mauritius to visiting the Taj Mahal at dawn before the crowds, island hopping in the Caribbean, and taking multiple European city breaks.

With my contacts book full to bursting and a wealth of first-person experience to translate into truly tailormade, magical holidays for clients, I decided the time had come to create my own company.

And so, Never A Wasted Journey was born.

CHAPTER SEVEN

Never A Wasted Journey

I was ready for a change, but what a change it was! I went from the stability of a regular wage to relying on what I booked each month simply to survive, from being surrounded by a team of people to working on my own (the staff Christmas party wouldn't be as much fun) and swapping my twenty-hour-a-week train journey for a twenty-second commute from my bedroom to the lounge. I knew it was a risky move, but I had the determination to succeed and prove my many doubters wrong.

I knew my company name was key, but 'Dan's Travel' or 'Salmon's Tours' didn't quite work. When I hit on 'Never A Wasted Journey', I knew this was exactly the message I wanted to get across, and it is something that I have continuously aimed to deliver over the nine years since. So, I registered the company, set up the website, created my social media accounts, and off I went.

It all began in a one-bedroom flat in Brentwood, Essex. I didn't have a single client or booking, just a sofa, a laptop, a kettle, and a cat. But I had already made one key decision: to take my business online rather than open a traditional brick-and-mortar agency. It saved upfront costs but also turned out to be the perfect business model for me. My busy clients didn't want to be restricted by time or location. Everyone has a mobile in their pocket, and that was all I needed to communicate with them.

I knew that business wasn't just going to land in my lap and spent my first few weeks scribbling away on my notepad, planning how I was going to stand out from the rest and what value I could bring to those who booked with me. I had access to the very best offers from suppliers, hotels, and airlines I had worked with for many years, so this wasn't a problem, but I wanted to include more.

I touched base with my contacts worldwide and negotiated added extras for my clients – for them to get something more than they would have got themselves at no additional cost and as a thank you for booking with me.

This is still something I always try to include – a bottle of champagne or chocolates in the room upon arrival, a romantic candlelit beach dinner or a relaxing spa treatment, to name a few. My suppliers also have the means to include room upgrades, early check-ins, or late check-outs where possible, too. These are the touches that make holidays as stress-free and special as possible.

I also knew I had another advantage over the large companies I'd worked for before: my clients would never feel like just another small fish in a large pond. They'd receive a truly personal service, with me working out-of-hours to fit in with their free time (5am calls before work starts for some, 10pm WhatsApp conversations once the kids are in bed for others, and even 2am emails from people who now book with me from different time zones). Those based closer have the option of home visits from me, and I've even dropped some clients off at the airport myself.

The Personal Touch
Only a few weeks after starting up, I had a text message at 7pm on a Sunday night from an individual who had been let down by the company he had booked with and was getting in touch to see if I could help. He was with six of his work colleagues on a staff incentive trip, a reward for a hard-working year. The trouble was that the company he had booked with had not done their homework and the group was now very disappointed, miles from home, having spent a fortune and been mis-sold a dream.

It was the early hours of the morning in Thailand and having got a good idea of what they would prefer, I told them to get some sleep and I'd have it all taken care of by the time they woke up. Keeping to my word, I worked until 3am to make their new travel arrangements. By the time they woke up and made their way down to breakfast, I had their travel documents sent across and chauffeur transfers waiting outside ready to take them to their new destination. My carefully crafted plans were exactly what they had in mind, and I now had six new clients!

Going above and beyond is just part of my job. One client realised his son had left his iPad on the plane while they were in their transfer to the hotel – by that evening, I had it delivered to them. Another client filled in a pre-arrival questionnaire for a safari lodge, jokingly mentioning his favourite drink was Irn Bru. Mission accepted – a single can of Irn Bru travelled by rail, road, and over-water, and to his surprise, it was waiting in his luxury tent when he arrived. I know that it's not the finer things in life that matter, but the finer details do, whether that's favourite drinks and bathroom products or nappies and a buggy for families travelling for the first time.

Going Viral
Despite all my hard work, the first year was tough. It was hard to get my name out there and convince people to have the confidence to book with me. It was here that my friends and family proved to be the biggest support I could have wished for. Wanting to help me where they could, they began booking their holidays with me, and I thanked them with all the additional extras I would organise for my high-spending clients.

This coincided with social media really taking off, and it was a godsend for me. One by one, they began posting pictures of themselves away on holiday, thanking me and putting photos up on their personal pages of the extras I had got them. Each time, my online followers increased and connections I had never met got in touch, curious as to how I could help them with their own travel plans – and get them that complimentary bottle of champagne in their room.

Word of mouth has been absolutely key for me. An individual who picked up on one of these posts was a well-known celebrity. (No, I can't name names – one of the reasons my clients book with me is that I understand how important their privacy is, so despite my gossipy tendencies, I never share details.) I had helped a mutual friend with a trip to the Maldives and this gentleman needed a little assistance with something special for his proposal trip.

After a sunset cruise with champagne and canapés, I organised the exclusive hire of an underwater restaurant, where a private chef cooked a seven-course meal of the couple's favourite dishes. As their special song played, two scuba divers swam by the window with a sign reading "Will you marry me?" Creating this unique proposal was thrilling enough, but then this celebrity posted a personal thank you to me, getting my name out there to his 500,000 followers.

We have built up a great relationship since and I've been lucky enough to create even more fantastic trips for him, but this had a huge impact on my business overnight. I now work with a number of other celebrities and sports personalities based in New York, Cape Town, Dubai, and beyond, tailor-making everything from spa escapes and city breaks to private islands and private jets. I have never looked back, and every enquiry still gives me the same buzz.

I've continued to expand my little black book of contacts, visiting many countries around the world, so I can offer personal recommendations. I've stayed at hidden gems in the Cotswolds and high-end luxury hotels in London. I've explored Paris, the Amalfi Coast, and Venice, where I organised my own proposal (my wife, Jo, said yes!). I've golfed in Tenerife, skied around the world (with no more injuries), cycled across the Golden Gate Bridge, ridden through Central Park in a horse-drawn carriage, helicoptered over the Grand Canyon, lazed in many a Caribbean Island hammock, honeymooned in the Maldives, explored Malaysia, toured through Vietnam, and trekked to see gorillas in Uganda.

Good Morning, Vietnam
These days, I've shaken off my accident-prone backpacker habits, and my travels are memorable for the right reasons. Vietnam was unforgettable from start to finish, beginning in Hanoi with a rickshaw ride and a street food tour. Once I'd plucked up the courage to step into the teeming traffic, I never looked back, people watching and

trying many delicious–and some more challenging; egg coffee, anyone?–traditional dishes. It was hectic, but so full of history, with beautiful gardens and architecture, an atmospheric old quarter and even the Ho Chi Minh Mausoleum, where you can visit the embalmed body of the beloved revolutionary leader. With a bit more travel expertise under my belt, I was well aware that the Hanoi Hilton is a former prison where the American military was held during the Vietnam War, not a luxury stay option.

I'd lined up an overnight cruise on an opulent junk boat through the waters of Halong Bay, where limestone pinnacles soar up from emerald waters like something out of a fairy tale. We stopped off to explore cave systems and floating fishing villages, and to swim in the bay before heading back on board for a cooking class and sunset cocktails on the top deck.

Next came the charming town of Hoi An, formerly a prosperous trading port attracting Chinese, Japanese, Dutch, Portuguese, and Spanish ships. We wandered among its lantern-filled narrow lanes, old merchant houses, market stalls, and boutique restaurants. You can get a tailor-made suit at the standard of Gucci for a tenth of the price delivered to your hotel within a day. Dining by the river was a highlight, although it turns out I still like a night out as much as I did in my younger years. Scrolling through my phone with a sore head the morning after, I discovered that not only did I get back to my hotel by jumping on the back of a moped, but while clinging on I serenaded the driver with my tone-deaf singing the entire ride. Poor man!

Our final stop was Saigon and what a change in style. A vibrant city with newly-built skyscrapers and a modern feel to it, but so much history hidden beneath the surface. It was here I learned more about the Vietnam War, visiting the Cu Chi Tunnels, a famous network of underground passages built to protect the Viet Cong guerrillas from attacks. Crawling through the tunnels, smashing my head at every turn and nearly wedging myself in, I was given a new appreciation for how tough and resilient they must have been. We also took a private boat up the Mekong Delta, meandering along the palm-lined waterways and passing secluded villages.

Unforgettable Uganda
Uganda was another highlight, making it onto my list of all-time favourite destinations. A loud crunching echoed through my ears as I attempted to get some sleep in my raised stilted room on the banks of the mighty Nile River in the middle of Murchison Falls National Park. No, I wasn't sharing with someone who had ordered room service for a midnight snack; this was hippo country and although by day they submerged themselves in the surrounding waters, by night they came to life and ventured on land to feed. An entire family seemed to have decided that the dining opportunities around my room were the restaurant of choice for the evening.

Hippos have the most powerful jaws in nature

and can crush a watermelon in one bite. Their feeding noise was deafening, but I certainly wasn't going to go out into the dark and complain to these notoriously tetchy creatures. I lay back and listened, with the noise making them seem so close that they could have even been in the room with me.

This was an adventurous trip and I had certainly already gotten close to nature as the itinerary promised. Once the sun rose and the hippos retreated into the river, I headed up to the main lodge for a well-deserved cup of tea—laced with sugar to combat the lack of sleep—and enjoyed my morning cuppa while sitting on the banks of the longest river in the world.

Soon, it was time to board a boat. Luckily, this time there was no need to cry, "man overboard!" As the mist rose over the tranquil waters, we floated upstream, spotting giraffes, crocodiles, monkeys, birdlife, and my good friends, the hippos. What a surprise awaited us as our boat pulled up on the bank – a pop-up mobile camp serving an unforgettable lunch just for us, in the middle of the wilderness and surrounded by incredible wildlife.

The fun wasn't over – we sailed on to where the Nile River gushed and tumbled through the throat of Murchison Falls, before trekking down into the depths of the gorge, where our ears were filled with the roar of the waters, the spray cooled our skin, and a rainbow formed overhead.

Our next stop was the Queen Elizabeth National Park, and I was lucky enough to spot the famous Tree Climbing Lions, who sleep away their day up in the branches. It was a rare thrill to see adults snoring away with their legs hanging down and the young cubs playing cheekily on the boughs, with only the odd fall off before mum scooped them up and they headed high above us once again. Staying in a tented camp within the park that night, we heard elephants passing close by on their way to bathe in the Ntungwe River, and in the morning, cheeky monkeys tried to snatch the fruit from our breakfast table.

Uganda's unrivalled highlight came when we reached the Bwindi Impenetrable Forest, home to half of the world's population of wild mountain gorillas. Keen to see these rare primates, we prepared to trek for hours through the ancient rainforest, but our luck was in. Barely fifteen minutes after setting off, our guides found the family of gorillas we were searching for. We slowly entered their habitat, keeping our heads bowed and making no sudden movements – we didn't want to scare or anger the majestic beasts. I looked up and came eye-to-eye with the Silverback running back and forward drumming his chest. This was his test, sizing me up, but I couldn't have been much competition as he soon sunk back down into the bamboo vegetation, satisfied we were no threat to his family. The older members of the group went about their activities as normal, foraging, grooming, and resting, while the young tumbled and rolled around playfully fighting with each other. The allocated hour we were permitted to spend with them rushed by, but I could have stayed forever.

The Perfect Pit Stop
Another bucket list trip came when I was invited as a VIP guest to the Singapore Grand Prix. My host was the owner of the rights to the Grand Prix itself and what an experience that was – the best seats in the house, hospitality, rooftop after-parties, the best restaurants, pit lane walks, and much more.

Seeing a trip like this from the other side as a client was such an inspiration and now, through my suppliers, I create fantastic sporting event experiences across the world, from F1 to the US Open golf or front-row seats at Wimbledon.

Now, I am proud to be able to offer you the chance to experience all of these bucket list trips for yourself. I've explored so many hidden corners of this world and I'm passionate about sharing what I know with my clients. My contacts are the best in the industry and no matter where you want to go, I can help you create your dream holiday.

CHAPTER EIGHT

Wow-Factor Experiences

My first-hand experiences have been an incredible perk of the job, but they've also allowed me to offer things that simply aren't available through traditional booking channels. To be honest, anyone can book a low-budget flight or hotel, and these give me little opportunity to add value. But move into the luxury sphere, and I come into my own – here's where my experience and expertise are the keys to secret doorways, unlocking experiences you'd never find via Google, and will treasure for years to come.

Here's just a taste of what I can offer:
- A 10km running tour with an ex-Olympian in Rome.
- A private samurai sword lesson with the lead choreographer from the Kill Bill movies in Japan.
- Dancing under the Northern Lights with a private DJ at a pop-up camp on a remote glacier in Iceland.

- Skiing with an Olympic Team in Canada.
- Sunrise yoga at the top of the Empire State Building in New York.
- The ultimate pub crawl by private jet through the Australian outback.
- Viewing marine life below the waves by chartering an underwater submersible in Antarctica.
- Afternoon tea with Royalty in India.
- Front row tickets to Paris Fashion Week.
- Navigating your own America's Cup high-speed racing yacht through San Francisco Bay with the help of an experienced captain and crew.
- A private dinner with cast members from the best shows on Broadway.
- Pit lane visits or mingling with F1 drivers during a Grand Prix, plus prime viewing and access to the most exclusive parties afterwards.
- Rolls-Royce adventures through the Scottish Highlands.
- Exclusive hire of your own wilderness retreat in the middle of Finnish Lapland and the chance to meet Santa himself in his log cabin home, bake cookies with his elves, feed reindeer, and enjoy a husky safari.
- A private dinner and helicopter tour of Robben Island in Cape Town with the former guard to Nelson Mandela.
- Sleeping in hammocks under star-filled skies in Belize, next to the second-longest barrier reef in the world. Hone your survival

skills, learn to catch, gut and cook fish, and how to turn seawater into freshwater.

This is just the start. I love a challenge, so whatever your travel dream is, I'll work to make it a reality.

After many years of hard work, I have single-handily grown Never A Wasted Journey into a company that sells millions of pounds worth of holidays each year, with clients all over the world. Within my first three years of starting, I was overwhelmed to be named 'Best New Agent' and 'Best Tourism Service', and to receive an 'Outstanding Achievement Award' and an 'Excellence in Customer Service' award at events throughout my home county of Essex.

In 2016, my success continued on a national platform. I couldn't believe it; never in my wildest dreams did I think I would be suited and booted, attending invite-only ceremonies (at the Natural History Museum and BAFTA to name a few) as a nominee and against some of the industry's very best agents. Dreams do come true; I was named 'Leisure Agent of the Year' by Travel Weekly, the UK's number one travel trade publisher.

Having spent many nights watching *Dragon's Den* from the comfort of my own home, I was stunned to discover I had found my way onto a certain Dragon's radar and Mr Theo Paphitis had chosen Never A Wasted Journey as one of his favourite small businesses in 2017. I received special recognition at the House of Lords, being named one of the top 100 Small Businesses in the UK. In 2018, I was a finalist in the 'Young

Entrepreneur of the Year' category at the British Travel Hall of Fame Awards, which recognises the highest achievers in the travel industry. Previous inductees include Thomas Cook, Sir Richard Branson, and the founder of the low-cost airline EasyJet, Sir Stelios Haji-Ioannou, so I was in stellar company.

And in 2019, I was recognised among 230 of my industry peers at a glittering ceremony at Rosewood London, where TTG Media named me Luxury Travel Designer of the Year. These awards left me speechless, but they also gave me the confidence to push on further and see exactly how far I could go.

The Biggest Challenge Yet
I was on the up, but they do say life is a rollercoaster, and my ascent was soon to come to a dramatic stop, before hurtling downwards. I had experienced catastrophic events in the travel industry before, but the Covid-19 pandemic was something else, bringing the world to a complete standstill. The wall of heat as the plane door opens, the adrenaline rush as you slalom down the slopes, the chinking of glasses as you drink a sundowner by the sea – all of these became distant memories. Flights were grounded, hotels closed, cruise ships floated passenger-less, and the travel bans began to bite. Close to 90% of the world's population experienced travel restrictions and an estimated 25 million aviation jobs and 100 million travel and tourism jobs were at risk, with between five and seven years' worth of industry growth lost.

I'm not downplaying the immediate health risks

of Covid. Having caught it myself, I know how unpleasant it can be, and I also know friends and family who have sadly lost those close to them. But it also had a catastrophic effect on my business. There's no doubt that the travel industry was one of the hardest hit, with many job losses and company closures, not to mention the severe impact on communities around the world that rely heavily on tourism.

I was one of the lucky ones in comparison, and rather than feel sorry myself, I kept myself busy – offering free advice to people about their travel plans (even if they hadn't booked with me), keeping my followers on social media constantly updated with the latest changes, and simply picking up the phone to check in and make sure my clients were ok. I was determined to do the right thing by my customers, so I refunded every single penny of two years-worth of bookings and survived on no income throughout the pandemic, while at the same time working free of charge to make many amendments when people simply were unable to travel.

I put myself in my clients' shoes and offered a full refund within a fortnight for those who couldn't get away. Once travel slowly started to open up again, I researched all the Foreign, Commonwealth and Development Office protocols for each destination, the testing and vaccination requirements, and the forms that needed to be completed for every booking. (Those many, many forms still haunt me). While others who had booked for themselves were turning up to hotels that weren't open, I kept on top of every update on behalf of my clients, acting quickly to get them home before any travel bans meant they'd be stranded or have a quarantine sentence to serve in an airport hotel upon their return.

With social distancing in mind, I pre-booked the limited number of restaurants, spa treatments, and kids' club spaces, so there would be no disappointments while away. Many once-in-a-lifetime trips or special occasions were re-booked and re-booked again, but I never once charged a change fee to do so and even negotiated with my partnered suppliers for their new holidays to be booked again at no additional cost. While many companies were hiking up prices, I was calling in favours and absorbing costs where I could. I always want to do the right thing, and this situation was no different. I never once tried to convince anyone to travel if they weren't ready, I was just there at the end of the phone to advise and be honest.

With people craving privacy and to escape the crowds, I have never made so many private jet bookings in my life. There are so many elements I can offer to make travel safer and more exclusive; luxury chauffeur transfers, meet and greet assistance and security fast track at airports, the opportunity to have bags picked up from people's homes and delivered to their hotels, exclusive villas and private island stays, plus an experience that many aren't aware of – the chance to have a 'private jet experience' even with a commercial flight, with access to an exclusive terminal away from the crowds and a driver taking you right up to the doors of your aircraft.

Working closely with my trusted partners, I was able to tear up the rule book and offer complete flexibility – holding flights off so we could monitor the next government travel roulette updates, offering full refunds with no questions asked should it not be possible to travel, and the chance for people to change their minds with no financial penalties during such an uncertain time.

While I considered my efforts just another day in the office, I was so thrilled and proud to find I was included in the list of the Top 30 Most Inspiring and Influential in Luxury Travel in 2021 by Carrier Holidays. Carrier is one of the very best luxury operators in the UK and the list was designed to "pay homage to inspiring business leaders, exceptional travel designers and small companies who, despite the challenges of 2020, have continued to deliver outstanding levels of service and support to their clients."

Aspire, the leading luxury travel trade media brand, named me Travel Advisor of the Year, reflecting my level of service throughout the pandemic. I also appeared in The Independent, being named one of the Best of British Businesses throughout this period.

I am so thankful for each award I have won on my journey so far. I mention them not to show off, but to show that hard work does pay off. I would never have thought that when I was sleeping with one eye open, watching cockroaches scurrying across the floor of a hostel, that I would be where I am today. I will continue to offer the very best levels of service and experiences I can until my last breath, and I look forward to what the future brings.

CHAPTER NINE

The Future of Travel

The future? Now, I know there is still a long way to go for the travel industry, but at the time of writing this, clear skies are starting to appear after the storm, and I'm seeing a number of key trends appearing. Health and wellbeing travel is booming (I'm booking personalised therapy and diet programmes for some clients), and there's a real desire to experience the great outdoors, whether that's the French Alps or the National Parks of the USA.

The slowdown of the pandemic has also motivated many to approach travel differently, more mindfully, with more consideration for the planet. Clients are staying for longer in a destination, buying local or supporting wildlife projects. In parts of Africa, the decimation of tourism has led to a huge increase in illegal poaching, so a safari holiday is a palpable way to help protect endangered animals. Meaningful experiences whilst away on holiday will last long after returning home, helping to improve the lives of future generations, whether that's by helping to build a local school or replenishing endangered coral reefs.

Covid has proved how short life can be and holidays are now more meaningful than ever before. The demand for bucket-list travel has boomed with people wanting to get excitement and adventure back into their lives. There are also now more multigenerational travel enquiries, with families wanting to make up for lost time with their nearest and dearest. Solo travellers are keen to get out into the wider world once again and having got through isolation alone are now feeling more confident than ever before.

But challenges remain. There may be last-minute changes, and with so many having been let down by their previous means of booking a holiday, people now feel they'd like a helping hand. Booking with me makes your life easier. I offer a seamless trip, complete flexibility, and financial protection. I can give you the confidence to put that 'Out of Office' autoresponder on and get back out there to enjoy the world.

I can help with almost any type of holiday. Read on for inspiration or get in touch and I'll create any bespoke itinerary you may have in mind.

Mr & Mrs
Private island retreats make the most magical couple's escape. Enjoy a Robinson Crusoe feel with all life's luxuries in the Seychelles or the Caribbean.

LGBTQ+
Take an adventure where all are welcome. Explore New Zealand by helicopter, landing on remote glaciers and wild beaches to enjoy a gourmet picnic complete with the finest wines and shellfish you've just caught.

Proposals
I'll work with you to create the most romantic setting imaginable. You want to dive to the bottom of a Polynesian lagoon and discover your special token of love in a giant clam shell? It can be done!

Young at Heart
How about the ultimate pub crawl, travelling through the Australian Outback from pub to pub by private jet?

Families
I know quality time is just as important as interconnecting rooms and an incredible kids club, so I can suggest family flamenco lessons, joining safari rangers on an anti-poaching patrol, or even a Caribbean Treasure Hunt sailing adventure, following the clues on a map. Or make Christmas special at a private wilderness retreat in Finnish Lapland where reindeer roam and Santa is waiting.

Spa
Select a hotel so remote it can only be approached by water, then visit a hilltop spa with views of the Vietnam Sea and the mountains for a bamboo massage, or a workout in the jungle gym.

Villa
Rooftop helipads, private art collections, underground wine caves, fleets of supercars, and celebrity chefs and international DJs on call – I can book you the world's most opulent villas, castles, riads, and private islands, so you feel like rockstars or royalty.

Honeymoon
Kick back on a white sand beach in Polynesia, staying in the former sanctuary of movie star Marlon Brando, or take the ultimate safari, sleeping in a stilted 'bird's nest' suite as Kenya's big game wanders below.

Special Celebration
Let me tempt you and your guests with exclusive use of a private Venetian palazzo overlooking the Grand Canal where you can throw your own Masked Ball, complete with spectacular performers and fine cuisine.

For the Love of Tea
Always wanted to learn the secrets of tea? Go on an extraordinary journey through China to meet the growers of the world's most expensive tea before pouring yourself a heavenly cup in the mythical Shangri-La.

Wine Lovers
Helicopter hop between South Africa's most awarded vineyards, tour the medieval wine cellars

and tunnels underneath Il Borro in Tuscany, or have breakfast with kangaroos in South Australia before enjoying owner-led tastings in boutique wineries.

Mindfulness
Send your mind on vacation as well as your body – where better to practice yoga than with a leading guru among the temples of India?

Adventure
I can charter submersibles that will take you beneath the waves to witness Earth's greatest marine migration or if you are feeling the adrenaline surge, why not skydive at the North Pole?

Sports Enthusiasts
Enjoy spectacular views of the circuits with indulgent Grand Prix hospitality packages including gourmet food, world-class wines, exclusive pit lane tours, and VIP entry into private Formula 1 after-race parties.

Rail
Sweep through the Canadian wilderness on board the Rocky Mountaineer, sip tea poured by your butler as the Maharajas Express crosses India or enjoy Peru in more comfort than I did on the Belmond Andean Explorer. Plan ahead for 2025, when luxuriously refurbished carriages from the original Orient Express will make the Paris-Istanbul journey.

Sailing
Whether you're a seasoned sailor or a beginner, I'll find the right ship for you to enjoy the breezes of the Caribbean, Greece, or Indonesia. Board the first true superyacht in the Galapagos and swim with penguins or anchor your private charter in the Maldives and dive with whale sharks.

Wellness
If you want to train at the Balinese retreat where Daniel Craig prepared for the rigours of playing 007, I can help. But I also understand wellness is about more than fitness. Medi-spas, including Sha Wellness in Spain and Austria's Lanserhof, host world-class experts in dealing with all aspects of health, whether you're recovering from long Covid or struggling with the effects of menopause.

Cruise
Enjoy the luxury of only having to unpack once and travelling in style from one fascinating destination to another – or even right round the world! See the

wonders of the Nile from an all-suite ship, enjoy champagne and caviar in the Caribbean surf, or explore Antarctica in six-star luxury from a ship with its own submarine.

Why Travel?
Unlike material things, experiences stay with us no matter what. And nothing packs in unforgettable, varied experiences like travelling. It's the best way to unplug from the pushes and pulls of daily life, helping us to forget about our problems, frustrations, and fears. It allows us to explore new places, cultures, cuisines, traditions, and ways of living that we could never experience at home.

To do this, we have to step out of our comfort zone and experience new things, helping us to grow on a personal level. Each journey brings its own unique challenge to overcome. For me, in my earlier days, it was travelling solo, whereas now, thanks to my wonderful wife Jo and our three children Harrison, Hendrix and Savannah, it's working out a formula to keep the kids entertained on a twelve-hour flight.

Travel gives you the opportunity to build friendships and connections with people all around the world. Whether you find yourself in a hotel bar or on an excursion, you can easily connect over food, new places, music, and culture. We also often have similar interests and values, making the conversation flow more easily. Even if we meet someone for just a few days, the memories can last a lifetime. They may even open doors to new possibilities in our future life.

If you don't venture far or often, it is hard to fully comprehend the world. Being exposed to varied cultures allows us to become open-minded and understand that despite looking different, we share the same hopes and dreams. These similarities are what bring us together.

CHAPTER TEN

Don't Waste Your Journeys

Holidays are a large investment of time and money, and so a disastrous or even merely disappointing trip is a huge blow. I always ask my customers exactly what they want from their holiday, and then aim to exceed their expectations. Why don't my competitors offer what I do? It's hard! Rather than just seeing each booking as an economic value, I take my time to get to know exactly what people want from their holidays, then use my skills, network, and knowledge to offer that perfect break away.

The travel experience with Never A Wasted Journey starts from the first email or call. With my partnered suppliers worldwide (who are the best of the best), I'm able to offer exclusive offers and save your precious time, but I like to take it further than that. I encourage my clients to think beyond the obvious, traditional ideas and, with access to a plethora of choices, can suggest opportunities that are just not available with standard booking routes.

I also make sure every tiny detail is taken care of, from correct documentation and pre-booking plane seats to interconnecting rooms, kids' club reservations, car hire, ski instructions, golf tee times – all included as a complimentary service with every booking.

I keep in touch all the way through to departure, arranging final balance payments, delivery of documents, and simply being available to answer any questions. Once you're away, you have my personal contact, so you can message on WhatsApp to make a last-minute dinner reservation or a relaxing spa treatment for later in the afternoon. If anything goes wrong, you can contact me 24 hours a day and I'll act quickly to rectify any possible issues. I've always got your back!

Once you return home, I love to know how a trip went, so I'll follow up to hear all about it (both good and bad points), and then I'm on hand once again to help with the next holiday. Once you've booked with me, you are part of my travel family, and I'll keep you updated with the latest travel trends, offers, and hotel openings, giving you the opportunity to make the most out of your holidays for years to come.

To discuss your own travel plans, please do get in touch, I would love to hear from you:
www.neverawastedjourney.com

About The Author

Dan Salmon is a leading travel design expert and multi-award-winning specialist in worldwide luxury holidays. Introduced to travel from an early age by his mum, Linda, Dan is a family man who is inspired by his wife, Jo, and three beautiful children, Harrison, Hendrix, and Savannah.

With a passion for travel and an unbeatable black

book of worldwide contacts, Dan provides jaw-dropping travel experiences for his clients. From chartering a yacht around the Sea of Cortez to camping on a glacier in Iceland, Dan goes above and beyond creating unbeatable experiences and memories that last a lifetime.

Regularly recognized for his work in the travel industry, here are some of Dan's recent accomplishments:

- Top 30 'Most Inspiring and Influential in Luxury Travel'
- Top 100 Small Businesses in The UK
- Travel Agent of the Year 2017, 2018
- Luxury Travel Designer of the Year 2019, 2020
- Travel Advisor of the Year 2021
- Chosen by BBC Dragons Den star Theo Phapitis as one of his favourite small businesses

Get in touch with Dan today and start planning the holiday of your dreams:
- Website: www.neverawastedjourney.com
- Email: Reservations@neverawastedjourney.com
- Instagram: @never_a_wasted_journey
- Twitter: @NAW_journey
- Facebook: Never A Wasted Journey
- Linkedin: Dan Salmon

My Little Heart Warrior

Throughout all that I have experienced in life, the one thing that has changed me more than anything has been the strength of my daughter Savannah, and so this book is dedicated to her, as well as Harrison and Hendrix, who have been the very best caring and protective older brothers.

A baby scan should be full of joy and excitement, but for us, after twenty minutes of silence, we were told there might be a problem with her heart.

What do you mean? Is our baby going to survive? What happens next? All these questions raced through our minds.

All we could do, though, was wait for another scan that was booked at the University College of London Hospital (UCLH).

After weeks of worry and Googling what it could possibly be (probably the worst thing we could have done), the day arrived, and we nervously made our way up to London. I'd heard many stories about the doctors from Great Ormond Street Hospital (who were meeting us at UCLH) being the best of the best, and now I can personally vouch for them being exactly that.

We were sadly told that she had a heart condition called 'Tetralogy of Fallot', and our world came crashing down around us.

For those who aren't familiar, TOF is where, due to four heart defects, infants have a lack of oxygen-rich blood reaching the body. The heart defects include:

Not getting enough oxygen to the lungs due to an underdeveloped/damaged Pulmonary Valve.

VSD (a hole in the heart)

An overriding aorta (in the wrong place)

A thickened right ventricle muscular wall (where the heart is working in overdrive)

For the remainder of the pregnancy, we had regular scans, check-ups, and unbelievable support. The good news was that they hoped she would not need surgery straight after delivery. And that was, indeed, the case as she entered the world, screaming the hospital down (and something that tends to still crop up to this day, reminding me who's the boss), but with no immediate worries.

The months that followed included regular home visits from nurses and further appointments at GOSH to keep a close eye on her. My wife and I didn't get much sleep, sleeping with one eye and ear open.

The next obstacle we were hit with was a situation known as 'Blue Spells'. For any other parent who has gone through this, it isn't nice, but something we were told to expect. Savannah would get shortness of oxygen in her blood that led to her skin turning a blueish colour, her breath getting faster, extreme tiredness, and even becoming unresponsive.

We had to go through a few of these spells during this period, late night ambulance call-outs, and trips to A&E. This eventually meant she needed an operation at just four and half months old; she had to undergo open heart surgery to treat her condition.

We nervously waited, with Savannah in her little gown, ready for her operation. Building up the courage to what faced us, one hour passed, then another, and another, until we were told her operation had to be cancelled last minute due to another child needing to have an urgent heart replacement. Even though this was a big play with our emotions, we completely understood. Having sadly witnessed the many poorly children under their care, we were ok to wait.

After an overnight stay, we were back with Savannah in her little gown again and waited for her to be called through. The time came, and we had expected it to last a few hours, but due to a couple of complications, it ended up lasting six. Nothing can prepare you for the agonising wait, but we finally got a phone call to say the operation had been a success.

The relief was unimaginable, and we rushed to see her in intensive care while wanting to give the doctor the biggest hug he'd ever received. We thought we were prepared for what to expect, but seeing your baby swollen and connected to drainage tubes, a ventilator, and drips, is beyond difficult.

A warning alarm went off, and immediate panic kicked in once again, "Nurse, nurse!" I shouted louder and louder, but we soon learned this was the norm.

The aftercare was mind-blowing, from one of the nurses being next to her bed 24 hours a day, helping with her recovery and keeping a close eye on her, to the world-leading doctors who literally saved her life.

It is incredible how quickly children bounce back and how strong they are. After just eight days, she was coming home. The one thing they couldn't fully repair was her valve, so they did have to remove it. But amazingly, children can live without the need for this.

Just eighteen months later, we have recently had the good news that she will only need to be seen once a year, and although we will be keeping a close eye on her growing up and she will need another operation later in life (to replace her valve), apart from the scar on her chest, you wouldn't know she was a cardiac baby. She is now a very active, cheeky, sweet young lady whose strength has blown us away.

Before Savannah's situation came into our lives, we knew very little about heart problems, so this isn't a plea for sympathy but a story I wanted to share to hopefully raise awareness and to let anyone else going through a similar journey know that all can be ok.

As a thank you to all that Great Ormond Street Hospital has done for us, I will also be donating a percentage from every book sold to their charity so, as they did for us, they can continue to save the lives of many other children.

Thank you for being a part of this.

YOUR TRAVEL WISH LIST

Printed in Great Britain
by Amazon